WHERE'S THE MEERKAT? JOURNEY THROUGH TIME

ILLUSTRATED BY PAUL MORAN

WRITTEN BY JEN WAINWRIGHT

DESIGNED BY ANGIE ALLISON AND ZOE BRADLEY

Michael O'Mara Books Limited

Maxwell Meerkat's Great Invention

Maxwell Meerkat loves inventing things. Mostly, his genius ideas fall flat (he doesn't like to talk about the JetPack incident).

But this time, he's really on to something. He has spent days tinkering with switches and levers, and his masterpiece is finally ready to show to the family. The clever little meerkat has made a TIME MACHINE!

As he puts the finishing touches to the machine, he looks up to see his family are all running towards him. Oh no! Fearsome falcon Kevin is up to his old tricks again. Kevin is actually vegetarian, but he loves swooping down from the sky and scaring the meerkats and their friends just for the fun of it. Poor little Roger, the squirrel from next door, is being chased, too.

Suddenly, Maxwell's sister Frankie jumps into the time machine. One by one, Maxwell's family and Roger follow her and are zipped away through time. Kevin's not giving up the chase that easily – he leaps in after them. There's nothing for it, Maxwell will have to join them, and hope he can control his latest invention ...

The meerkats, Kevin and Roger are off on an amazing adventure through history! Can you spot all twelve of them in every picture? Tick them off as you find them.

Really eagle-eyed searchers can use the special 'Spotter's Checklists' at the back of the book, where there's more fun stuff to find and tick off in every picture.

Individual Profiles

Find out a bit more about each of the crazy critters on this historical adventure.

Name: Miranda

Will go down in history for: Her memoirs, which shed 'a warm and funny light on life in the warren'.

Name: Albert

Will go down in history for: Being the oldest meerkat to compete in the desert decathlon.

Name: Sofia

Will go down in history for: Her first range of couture gowns on the Meer Katwalk.

Name: Frankie

Will go down in history for: Campaigning for more recognition for female desert dwellers, along with her friends Sylvia and Emmeline Mongoose.

Name: Samson

Will go down in history for: The discovery of a new, bright purple desert flower, which he will name Samsonius.

Name: Kevin

Will go down in history for: A winged reign of terror. Or a career in stand-up comedy.

Name: Florian

Will go down in history for: His hilarious interview style on the TV chat show 'Florian Meets ...'.

Name: Raoul

Will go down in history for: Selling out the burrow's arena with his thrash metal band Snakes 'n' Scorpions.

Name: Matthew

Will go down in history for: Opening the first meerkat-run restaurant to get a prestigious 'Crunchy Cricket' award.

Name: Maxwell

Will go down in history for: His time machine, later christened the Maxwell-O-Matic.

Name: Hannah

Will go down in history for: Her 'Mongoose and Meerkat' series of oil paintings.

Name: Roger

Will go down in history for: Being the first squirrel to finish the infamous 'Big Bug Burger' at Katz Diner.

King Henry's Court, England
1535

King Henry VIII loved feasting. In one year alone, more than 8,000 sheep and 2,000 deer were cooked and eaten at his court.

The travellers have arrived in the middle of a banquet. There are several courses and almost 1,000 hungry mouths to feed. There are deer and rabbit pies, roasted peacocks, wild boar, sweet glazed fruit and pastries.

Tick off all ten meerkats, Kevin and Roger as you spot them.

Delphi, Greece
861 BC

The travellers have landed on the slopes of Mount Parnassus, Greece. They've come to see The Pythia, a famous Oracle. It is said she hears the words of the God, Apollo.

People come to The Pythia to ask questions about their future. Farmers are asking her when they should plant their crops, but Hannah plans to ask what song she should sing at her audition for The Meerkat Factor.

Tick off all ten meerkats, Kevin and Roger as you spot them.

Colorado, USA
1881

Yee ha! The travellers have touched down in the Old West. There's a new sheriff in town, and a notorious outlaw on the run.

Albert has taken to calling everybody 'partner', which gets on everyone's nerves, while Roger is displaying a surprising level of skill at cards inside the local saloon.

Hopefully Maxwell will catch the cheeky squirrel before he consumes too much of a potent drink called sarsparilla and gambles away their precious time machine!

The River Nile, Egypt
2500 BC

The meerkats have landed on the banks of the Nile, and it's time to go hunting – Ancient Egyptian style.

Kevin needs to watch out for the pointed throwing sticks that keep zipping through the air. Those hunters have impressive aim! Samson tries his hand at a spot of fishing, but after three failed attempts at striking with a spear, and one embarrassing fall into the river, he leaves it to the professionals.

Tenochtitlan, Mexico
1448

Having left the shelter of the time machine, everyone is amazed at the noise and bright colours around them. They've landed in the capital city of the Aztec empire, and it's a busy place to be!

Roger is starving and heads to market to practise his haggling skills and get his paws on some tasty maize. Raoul is more interested in the Aztec warriors. The really mighty ones are dressed as jaguars and eagles. Raoul hates fashion, but this is a style he can really relate to!

The Alps
218 BC

Matthew and Sofia are sulking. They don't know where they are, and it's freezing cold. Sofia is bored and Matthew is hungry. But wait ... are those ELEPHANTS? Things are about to get a lot more exciting!

The time machine has taken them to a pass in the Alps, where General Hannibal is crossing with his army (and his elephants) to take the Romans by surprise. He has certainly surprised the meerkats! They can't believe they're seeing real live elephants high up in the mountains.

London, England
1879

Roll up! Roll up! It's market day in Victorian London, and the air is filled with new sights, sounds and smells. Kevin (who has always rather fancied himself as an English gent) is strolling around in his top hat and cane, admiring the stalls.

Raoul, on the other hand, is keeping his ears open for examples of people using 'cockney rhyming slang'. He wants to learn this London dialect to confuse his sisters later, although at the moment he's having trouble understanding it himself.

☐ ☐ ☐ ☐ ☐ ☐ ☐ ☐ ☐ ☐ ☐ ☐ ☐

The Jurassic Period
150 million years ago

Oops! This time Maxwell really has gone too far – too far into the past that is. Miranda's about to complain about how hot and sticky it is, when she sees that this is the least of her worries. They're surrounded by giant dinosaurs!

There's Triceratops with his horny head, and spiny-backed Stegosaurus. Even the little dinos look ready to chomp a tasty meerkat snack.

The Taklamakan Desert, 1273

The sun is beating down on the meerkats as they join a caravan of merchants and camels on the 'Silk Road', which connects China in the east and Rome in the west.

The caravan winds its way through deserts and mountains taking tapestries, silks, spices, precious stones, gold, silver and pottery to market. Sofia has her eye on a bolt of deep violet silk, but the camel carrying it has a look in his eye that makes her nervous. Getting spat on by an angry camel wouldn't do her image any good.

☐ ☐ ☐ ☐ ☐ ☐ ☐ ☐ ☐ ☐ ☐ ☐

New York, USA
1924

The meerkats are ready to show off some serious dance moves. They've landed in one of New York City's most famous jazz clubs, and everything is just swell!

Miranda and Albert are doing a fast-paced dance called the 'Lindy Hop', and showing the youngsters how it's done. Samson has discovered the fashionable footwear of the 1920s – black shoes with white cloth covers over them, called 'spats'. He thinks they're terrific, and plans to take several pairs back home to wear at the warren.

The Caribbean Sea
1717

Shiver me timbers! The time machine has landed on the *Queen Anne's Revenge* – the ship of the fearsome pirate, Blackbeard! He's just stolen this ship from the French, and is ready for some more looting.

Kevin gets stuck right in, swashing and buckling in no time. The meerkats can hear him yelling 'Ahoy me hearties!' and 'Avast, ye scurvy landlubber!' from all the way across the ship. Frankie doesn't want to make him angry, but she can't help giggling at how silly he sounds.

Provins, France
1440

The thunder of hooves and the clanking of armour fills the air as the time travellers arrive at a jousting tournament. Knights ride along the dusty arena and try to knock each other off their horses with long pointed sticks called 'lances'. The winner gains glory, honour, riches and, possibly, the favour of a beautiful noblewoman.

Matthew and Florian are hooked. They plan to hold a tournament when they get back to the warren, involving mongooseback riding and fearsome twig lances.

Berlin, Germany
1989

When they see where they've landed, Albert, Miranda and Florian understand that this is an important event. They're seeing the fall of the Berlin Wall – a huge, fortified structure that separated East Berlin from West Berlin for almost 30 years.

Despite his age, it's Albert who gets stuck in. He gets his paws on a wheelbarrow and is soon shifting rubble from one place to the next. Matthew and Frankie are busy 'helping', which means taking turns to sit in the barrow and go for a ride!

Lindisfarne, England
793

Oh no! The time machine has landed on a tiny island off the coast of England in the middle of a Viking raid!

Samson's secretly rather impressed by the fearsome Scandinavian warriors and their sleek longship. Miranda, on the other hand, is focusing on the fact that they seem to be setting everything on fire and cursing a lot. She doesn't appreciate impolite behaviour, and has set about fixing every Viking she comes across with one of her particularly hard stares.

☐☐☐☐☐☐☐☐☐☐☐☐

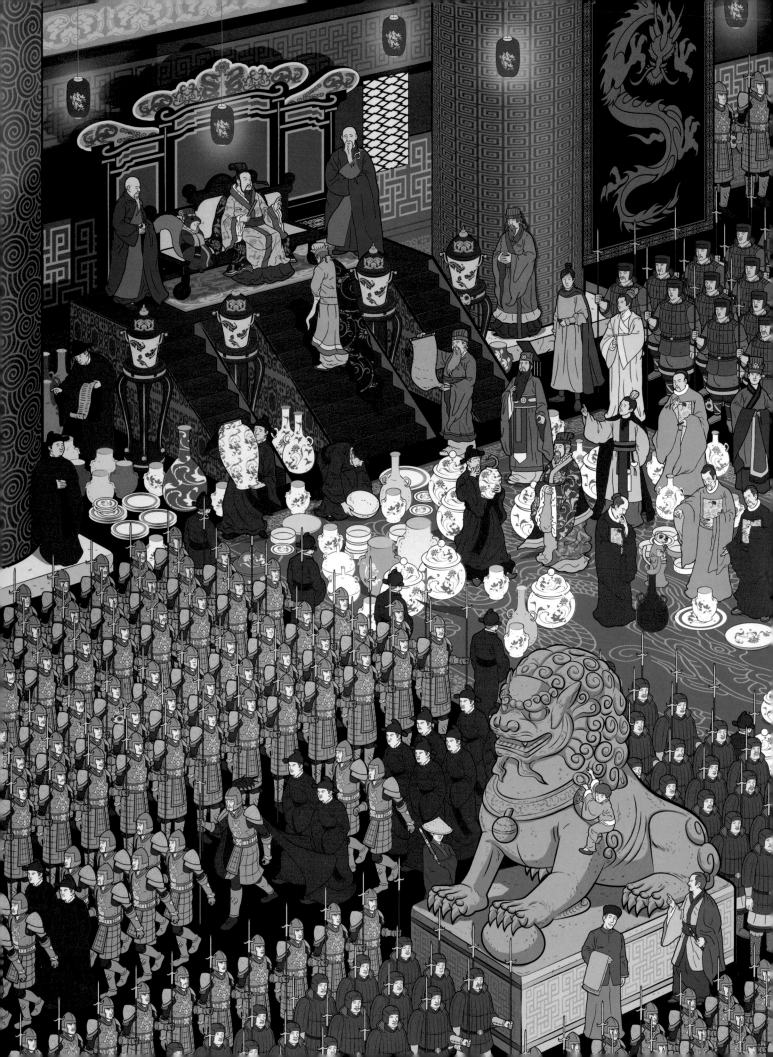

Beijing, China
1424

The travellers have landed in the magnificent home of the Chinese Emperor, known as The Forbidden City. Today is the Emperor's birthday, and many princes, dukes and officials have come to worship and pay their respects, bringing lavish gifts with them.

Miranda has fallen in love with a tiny, patterned vase. She can already imagine it on her dining table back at the warren, and she's plotting how to sneak it back with her without anyone noticing!

☐ ☐ ☐ ☐ ☐ ☐ ☐ ☐ ☐ ☐ ☐ ☐

Waterloo, Belgium
1815

This is not a safe place for the time machine to have landed! Kevin, Roger and the meerkats are slap bang in the centre of the Battle of Waterloo, where the French Emperor Napoleon is fighting armies from Britain, Germany, Holland, Belgium and Prussia.

Roger is putting on a brave face, but really he's terrified! He thinks he's getting away with it, but everyone can see the tip of his bushy tail quivering with fear.

Metropolis X300
3469

The time travellers have been sent zipping far into the future to a slick city of gadgets, robots and gleaming metal.

Maxwell feels completely at home, but the others are less comfortable. Hannah is struggling to master a hover scooter and is wobbling about in midair causing traffic jams. Florian keeps wandering under the Transportation Suction Tubes and squeaks with dismay when he's picked up, zoomed along inside the tubes at top speed and deposited somewhere else in town.

Answers

Spotter's Checklist

A waitress dropping pies ☐

A milkmaid with pails of milk ☐

Someone choking on their dinner ☐

An upside-down pig ☐

Someone being sick ☐

A man breakdancing ☐

A dog begging on its hind legs ☐

A maid carrying buckets of firewood ☐

Four roast chickens on the floor ☐

A woman throwing her drink over someone ☐

KING HENRY'S COURT, ENGLAND 1535

DELPHI, GREECE 861 BC

Spotter's Checklist

The Pythia, the priestess of the oracle ☐

A meditating woman ☐

A man with wings on his helmet ☐

A bodybuilder ☐

A woman reading a scroll ☐

A man with a trident ☐

A soldier whose helmet is on fire ☐

13 goats ☐

A man tripping up ☐

Someone with a headache from the mystic vapours ☐

Spotter's Checklist

- A man in a stripy scarf
- An undertaker
- A rider falling off a horse
- A man with a monocle
- The outlaw from the WANTED poster
- A woman with a bright pink fan
- A rooftop fist fight
- A gold miner with a pickaxe
- The sheriff (wearing a sheriff's star)
- A little girl wearing purple

COLORADO, USA 1881

Spotter's Checklist

- Mummies on the loose
- A man with a whip
- A broken oar
- A hunter's cat
- A fish in the face
- Handmaidens holding baskets
- Someone falling headfirst in the river
- Six hippos
- A man being chased by his prey
- Two hunters carrying an antelope

THE RIVER NILE, EGYPT 2500 BC

TENOCHTITLAN, MEXICO 1448

Spotter's Checklist

- A man-eating fish
- A purple feathered headdress
- A rampaging llama scattering baskets
- A blue-painted prisoner running away
- An eagle warrior testing his wings
- A woman reading a stone tablet
- A fat man in a gold necklace
- An angry kicking llama
- A man falling over backwards with a heavy sheaf of corn
- Three chatting women with elaborate hairstyles

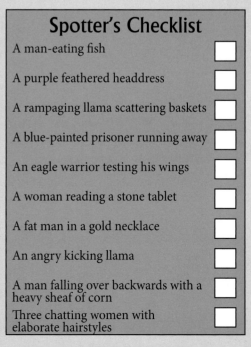

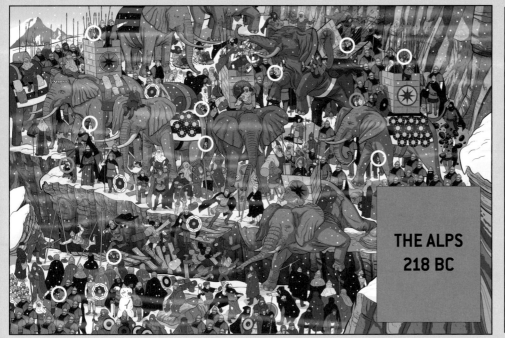

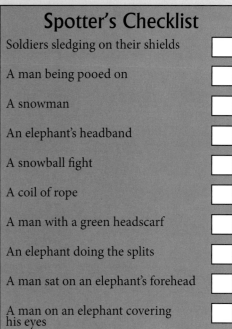

Spotter's Checklist

Soldiers sledging on their shields	☐
A man being pooed on	☐
A snowman	☐
An elephant's headband	☐
A snowball fight	☐
A coil of rope	☐
A man with a green headscarf	☐
An elephant doing the splits	☐
A man sat on an elephant's forehead	☐
A man on an elephant covering his eyes	☐

THE ALPS 218 BC

Spotter's Checklist

A rearing horse	☐
A one-man band	☐
A man riding an unusual animal	☐
A cat among the pigeons	☐
An angry policeman	☐
A clumsy chimney sweep	☐
A young pickpocket	☐
Two men on penny-farthing bicycles	☐
A detective with a magnifying glass	☐
A monkey dancing on a man's hat	☐

LONDON, ENGLAND 1879

THE JURASSIC PERIOD 150 MILLION YEARS AGO

Spotter's Checklist

A dino with a bright mohican	☐
A dinosaur relaxing on his back	☐
Five dragonflies	☐
A tiny dino climbing high	☐
A dino trampling on another's head	☐
Three flying dinosaurs	☐
A stegosaurus	☐
A triceratops	☐
An allosaurus	☐
Four green dinos wading in the water	☐

THE TAKLAMAKAN DESERT 1273

Spotter's Checklist

Two runaway camels ☐

A man being drooled on ☐

A man struggling to carry a large box ☐

A man holding a sword and a spear ☐

A mother giving her son an apple ☐

A girl travelling in a basket ☐

A stubborn camel that won't get up ☐

Someone having a drink ☐

A man being hit in the face by a treasure chest ☐

A boy in yellow trousers and a blue waistcoat ☐

Spotter's Checklist

A gangster with a gun ☐

A group photograph ☐

A woman who has fallen over dancing ☐

A woman sitting on a ledge ☐

A tuba player wearing a hat ☐

A waiter spilling his tray ☐

A man being pulled by his tie ☐

Someone being pushed down the stairs ☐

A dancer on stage with the wrong colour shrug ☐

A man who has messed with one of the bouncers ☐

NEW YORK, USA 1924

THE CARIBBEAN SEA 1717

Spotter's Checklist

A leg amputation – ouch! ☐

Someone using a mop as a weapon ☐

Some hanging heads ☐

A pirate wearing pink ☐

A toothy shark ☐

Blackbeard, with bows in his beard ☐

Ten green parrots ☐

A fearless female pirate ☐

Someone with a cannonball tied to his feet ☐

A bald pirate with a hook for a hand ☐

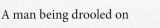

PROVINS, FRANCE 1440

Spotter's Checklist

A cheering king ☐

A witch ☐

A man with an arrow in his hat ☐

A man with an eyepatch ☐

An attacking hawk ☐

A woman with a basket of bread ☐

A jester on someone's shoulders ☐

A man eating a bread roll ☐

A knight pole-vaulting with his lance ☐

A knight in armour watching from the stands ☐

Spotter's Checklist

An Alsatian ☐

A woman on a pogo stick ☐

A man in a wheelbarrow ☐

Three cameras ☐

Someone falling off the wall ☐

A man holding a ladder ☐

A man juggling ☐

A woman with a pink bow in her hair ☐

Someone balancing on a bike saddle ☐

Someone getting in the way of a hammer ☐

BERLIN, GERMANY 1989

LINDISFARNE, ENGLAND 793

Spotter's Checklist

Jewellery for sale ☐

A woman making a pie ☐

A Viking being weed on by a pig ☐

A cunning use for rotten vegetables ☐

A Viking blowing a horn ☐

A boy riding a pony ☐

A barefoot woman running ☐

A Viking surprised by a fish ☐

A Viking buying a carved statue ☐

Someone falling headfirst into a cart of straw ☐

BEIJING, CHINA 1424

Spotter's Checklist

A snake in a vase ☐

A climbing child ☐

Smashing crockery ☐

A juggler ☐

Two women sharing a drink ☐

Three parasols ☐

A statue on the move ☐

Three men in conical hats ☐

An impressive balancing act ☐

Someone reading a tasselled scroll ☐

WATERLOO, BELGIUM 1815

Spotter's Checklist

Someone covering his ears ☐

A soldier with a slingshot ☐

A man playing the bagpipes ☐

A man getting his head bandaged ☐

Someone up to his middle in a puddle ☐

A man with two swords ☐

A gold cannon ☐

A man holding a bomb ☐

A man dropping a cannonball on his foot ☐

A soldier's hat being sliced in two with a sword ☐

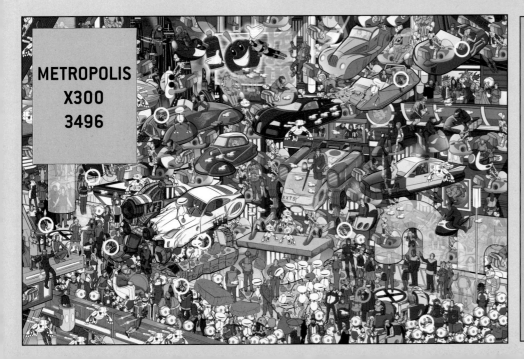

METROPOLIS X300 3496

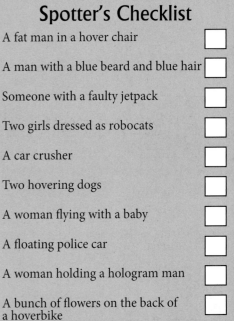

Spotter's Checklist

A fat man in a hover chair ☐

A man with a blue beard and blue hair ☐

Someone with a faulty jetpack ☐

Two girls dressed as robocats ☐

A car crusher ☐

Two hovering dogs ☐

A woman flying with a baby ☐

A floating police car ☐

A woman holding a hologram man ☐

A bunch of flowers on the back of a hoverbike ☐

Published in Great Britain in 2012 by Michael O'Mara Books Limited,
9 Lion Yard, Tremadoc Road, London SW4 7NQ

www.mombooks.com

A CIP catalogue record for this book is available from the British Library.

Hardback ISBN: 978-1-84317-804-0
Paperback ISBN: 978-1-84317-948-1

1 3 5 7 9 10 8 6 4 2

This book was printed in July 2012 by
Shenzhen Wing King Tong Paper Products Co., Ltd., Shenzhen, Guangdong, China

Papers used by Michael O'Mara Books are natural, recyclable products made from wood grown in sustainable forests. The manufacturing processes conform to the environmental regulations of the country of origin.